Trip Down Memory Lane:

Old Book for Old Thoughts

If ⟳ Then

BY DORIS A. BROOKS

Write It Out
PUBLISHING, LLC

Virginia Beach, Virginia

Contribution by Kiyanni Bryan, Write It Out Publishing LLC in the United States of America.

Illustrator: Trae Spears & Jason Josiah

Editor: Tamira K. Butler-Likely & Sheryl Johnson

ISBN: 978-1-7377484-7-2

First Printing:2022

Author: Doris Brooks

Virginia Beach, VA 23464

Destinyjoyj2@gmail.com

Dedication

I dedicate this book to the matriarchs of my family; Simon Daniels, my great-grandfather; Sarah and Bill (William) Daniels, my grandparents; Carrie Daniels Frazier, my mom; Hattie Daniels Gray, my aunt with whom I spent my happy childhood days running barefoot and playing in piles of recently raked leaves, and Billy William Henry Daniels, my uncle, brother, friend, and my hero who rode my sister and I through the leaves and mud holes on his bicycle.

I am looking down the long roads that have taken me to where I am now in life. God has been my Rock and my Shield.

Acknowledgment

I thank God for all the people who believed I could make this book interesting, hilarious, and maybe helpful in some haphazard way. One particular morning, He woke me up early, as He usually does, and had me think about how times, languages, and situations have changed over many years. He allowed me to think about how my forefathers and mothers did not have a formal education but yet wisdom and common sense reigned supreme in their reasoning, thinking, and their way of life. I did not nor could not have written these former babblings without the help of many others who have experienced the wisdom and superstitions, and at the time, they were sound doctrines.

I cannot remember everyone's name who has contributed to this book. I acknowledge my family, my friends, and my associates. I acknowledge that images used in this book are not my own.

Table of Contents

Looking Backward and Forward

This book arose from God's revelation
to me as I was meditating on other biblical
thoughts. In the middle of my meditating, I
began to think of my past. I thought of my
great-great and grandparents and how they
communicated and gave advice to their
family, friends, neighbors, and me. I
dedicate this book to the matriarchs of my
family; Simon Daniels, my great-
grandfather; Sarah and Bill (William)
Daniels, my grandparents; Carrie Daniels
Frazier, my mom; Hattie Daniels Gray, my
aunt with whom I spent my happy childhood
days running barefoot and playing in piles of
recently raked leaves, and Billy William
Henry Daniels, my uncle, brother, friend,
and my hero who rode my sister and I

through the leaves and mud holes on his bicycle. Most of the time, he deliberately made us fall off the handlebars of his bicycle into the mud just to get  my sister, Vera Brown Daniels (Dabbs), and I in trouble.

All these adventures taught me valuable life lessons that have kept me aligned with characteristics that have planted my feet on solid ethical and moral foundations. I cannot tell you what lessons I learned by being dumped into the mud, but Billy had fun seeing us covered from head to toe in it. Our children of today need a better connection with the values of their forefathers and foremothers who were not rich in material things but were rich in ethical values. They loved their families and their neighbors. If we had meat, our neighbors shared in that meat. Some of my childhood lessons, taught by my ancestors, were to help not hurt our neighbors. Our mission was to help them meet their physical and Spiritual needs. We were overjoyed in being a part of their lives. My foreparents shared what they had. They cried when their neighbors cried and mourned the loss of everybody's loved one. They would cook a large meal and take the meal and me to a "setting up" that lasted all night just to show their neighbors they shared in the loss of their loved ones. Neighbors were connected heart to heart and breast to breast, Spirit to Spirit. I did not always understand some of their logic back then, but as I became an adult, their teachings became fruitful in my everyday life of achieving and overcoming challenging positions by utilizing common sense and love for all God's creations.

My older parents were all professionals in their field of common sense. My grandfather should have been an astrologist. Why? The "boss man" of the farm always gave the farm workers a snack every day between early morning work time and dinner time (lunchtime). My grandfather would tell us what time of the day to do certain things, without a pocket watch.

He would look up at the sky and say, "Welp, it's 'bout time fer a snack." He knew it was 10 a.m. Then he would look at the sky and say, "Welp, it's time fer dinner" or "it's time fer supper." He even knew when a storm was about to begin, when there was not a cloud in the sky. My grandmother's name was Sarah. He would look up and say, "Sara, pick up that hoe and let's go to the house 'cause it's 'bout to rain." She would say, "Bill, how you know a storm is a coming 'cause I don't see no clouds in that sky?" He would say, "Alright, you stay, but I'm gone." He would pick up his hoe and head toward the house. The fields where we were working were about two miles from the house, it was a huge farm. When we got to the house, Grandpa would be sitting on the porch with a big smile on his face because he was dry and Grandma and the rest of us were as wet as a pole cat that had been thrown in a riber (river), so he said.

"A hoe is a hand tool used to remove weeds from between plants."

I have heard the voices of other people who have heard sayings from their foreparents, and I have included them in this book. I am thankful for their input. My friends and I have enjoyed sharing the "wisdom of proverbs" our great-grands, our grandparents, and sometimes, our parents, who have communicated valuable lessons to us down through the years. But, of course, some of those wisdom statements were followed with a good old-fashioned spanking—they called it a whipping—when we did not heed their warnings or sayings. In those days and times, we knew we had to be obedient to those who had the rule over us; that meant obedience to any grown-up, and especially obedience to our teachers. The worst whippings we would get was when the teacher reported to our parents that we were hardheaded and disobedient. Teachers knew every parent and where they lived and did not hesitate in reporting what their children were doing in school. In fact, the teacher would have a sit-down supper with the parents to discuss their children. Oh, how I hated that!

My family consists of many siblings, including my in-laws, and me. We enjoyed gathering around the table with a piled high plate of home-cooked food, with homemade biscuits or cornbread and molasses pudding, to talk about old times and the things we used to do as children. Unfortunately, most of the time, if not all the time, someone ended up getting a "beating" by our parents for the sneaky but playful and naughty deeds we had done to each other. They did not allow us to fight each other, and we had to be careful not to get too debatable with each other. It was a terrible sin and a disgrace to hit one of your siblings. The CIAs (our parents) would track down the perpetrators and immediate judgment was handed down on the very spot of the crime scene. The one time my two brothers, Howard and Leroy, got into an altercation with each other did not end well for one of them. Howard allowed Leroy to win. My mom caught them fighting and she put her hand on her hip and said, "Oh! So you want to fight now? Ok, if you want to fight, go out there and bring me three switches.

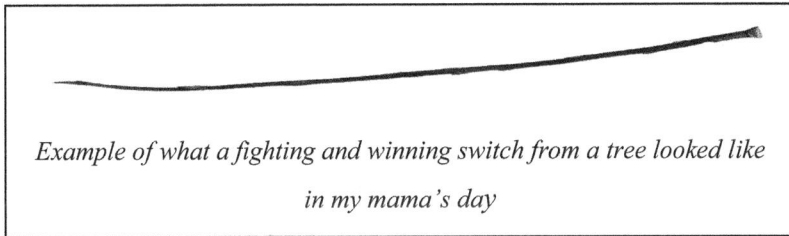

Example of what a fighting and winning switch from a tree looked like in my mama's day

One for each one of you and one for me. Now fight and the winner will get a beating from me." After that episode of Mom winning, none of us wanted to fight again.

Yes, our parents were farmers, but they could have worked for the CIA because they were the best private eyes, detectives, and investigators in the world. They could detect, without seeing the crime scene, which of the eleven children had committed what crime in or outside the house. The perpetrator would be given the opportunity to give the suspect up, but when the perpetrator would not admit to the crime, action was taken—a beating with a switch from the nearest tree or bush that the judge, our parents, ordered the perpetrator to pick from the bush—for the carrying out of our punishment. No one was put on probation because we had to work off the decisions the judges ordered by making us work harder in the fields after the beating. One example of the CIA's detection abilities comes to mind, when we were allowed to have cheese for Sunday morning breakfast. My parents would buy the cheese on Saturday when they went to the grocery store. The cheese was stored away safely in the refrigerator until the next morning. On Sunday morning, the cheese was carefully unwrapped to be distributed to each family member. On this particular Sunday morning, when the cheese was unwrapped, someone had taken a big bite out of the cheese.

The chief CIA investigator started inspecting to see who the culprit was that had bitten the cheese. All the suspects, all the children, were asked, "Which one of you bit this cheese?" Not one of us admitted to biting the cheese. He began to ask each one, "Did you bite the cheese?" Each suspect said, "No, it won't me." "OK then," he said. "All of you line up in a straight row." We had no choice but to follow orders. Then he said, "All of you grin and show your teeth."

He went from child to child and teeth to teeth with the cheese in his hand. When the teeth print on the cheese matched the shape of child's teeth who bit the cheese, he said, "It was you, you bit the cheese."

Needless to say that all of us children were scared for my sister Jeanette for biting the cheese. I will just say this, it was a long time before she wanted cheese again after the whipping she got. He said that he did not whip her for biting the cheese but whipped her for lying about it. Of course, we could not say "lying" because that was a bad word, so he said, "Telling a story about biting the cheese." There are many more incidents I could tell of how when one child got in trouble, all of us were in trouble. As adults, we look back on those days with lots of laughter, although it was not funny at the time of the incidents.

My great-grandparents and entire family were Christians who prayed and talked about the wondrous works of Jesus, yet my foreparents and other adults used to say and predict things that could or would happen in life or tell things that were beneficial or detrimental for a good life. I am not sure if what they communicated to us were biblical practices or something they made up along life's journey. Maybe the "wise" sayings and their insights were for entertaining since clans of families gathered often for conversations, food, and homemade corn liquor, without the knowledge of the children. I used to wonder what my grandmother meant when she would say to my grandfather, "Look at you; your eyes are as little as a field pea." Now, as an adult, she meant he was a little bit tipsy. Of course, the children had to play in other areas because children were not allowed to hear grown folk talking. After talking about "stuff" the children were not allowed to hear, they would call all of us together to tell us stories, especially ghost stories. Sometimes they told of something terrible that could happen in life and what to do to avoid mishaps. All of those sayings sounded mysterious and scary, and as children, we believed what they said and, therefore, did what they said to do. My grandfather, Bill, used to tell us stories of how he would drive the mules hooked to a wagon down the road past a graveyard.

When he looked back, he would see a man with no head sitting on the back of the wagon.

(Man waiting to jump off the wagon at the graveyard.)

As he approached the graveyard, the headless man would hop off the back of the wagon and go into the graveyard. As I got older and wiser, I used to ask myself how he could have been so heroic then. When the chickens were being disturbed on a dark night, he would wake my grandmother out of her sleep and say, "Sara, sump thing at the chickens." My grandmother would get out of bed, grab a flashlight, and go to the chicken coup to make sure the chickens were safe. She would kill the snake that tried to swallow the baby chicks, go back to bed and back to sleep as if nothing had happened. We had always had strong women who led the family, not saying the men did not take their rightful place in the family.

When I think of some of the "sayings" that seem to be gospel to some, as an adult, *I thought, how could they have all those "sayings" and still believe and trust in God?* But you may ask, "What does God have to do with anything? I say that because most of what they said was superstitious jargon. Of course, some older people still believe these things, but we discovered that most were rubbish as we grew older. My parents halted those old sayings of their parents that most of the time, defied logic. Now, you, as readers, have the opportunity to decide or decipher for yourselves the benefits of my childhood experiences. Now you have the opportunity to share in the teachings I was taught and was instructed to do and consider if those sayings could have added anything beneficial to our lives and not been detrimental to our adult thoughts.

The first memory of my grandmother was her praying after a hard day of cooking and working on the farm to feed a huge family. Just before going to bed, she would pray a short prayer, not a long, drawn-out prayer. She would get on her knees, fold her tired, wrinkled hands, and say, "Lord, have mercy on my soul." One night I asked her why she prayed that prayer. She told me that God's mercy was all we needed for everything we needed.

Today when I pray, I talk to God about a lot of things, but I end it by asking God to have mercy on my soul. I have witnessed the evidence of His mercy during my childhood while watching my grandparents work hard all year long, then to hear the owner of the farm say to them at the end of the year that they had not earned any money after all the crops were sold. "All the profits went toward what it took to farm for that year," they said. "You just broke even." I could see the hurt and disappointment on their faces,

but we never went without food to eat or clothes to wear. It wasn't much, but

God continued to show His mercy toward us during the next farming season. The sad thing about it was that they would hear the same story at the end of the next year. We did not have money to see a doctor when we got sick, but God had mercy on us. God's mercy still reigns!

I wrote these sayings randomly since I cannot remember when I heard them or who created them. Get ready to be entertained or enlightened!

I pray you will be able to decipher
each statement, then laugh when you realize
what the messages of some of these "old
sayings" were saying or teaching.

If a black cat passed in front of
your car while driving and she/he passed
from the right to the left, that was bad luck.
Then you must immediately make a cross on
your windshield with your pointer finger to
break the curse, or you must turn the car
around, go back where you started
originally, and go in another direction to
reach your destination. My sister-in-law,
Geraldine, told me that her aunt still
practices this saying. Now, what sense did
that action make? Note: After all, the poor

old black cat just wanted to get to the other side of the  road without getting killed. She probably was wondering to herself, *what's wrong with those humans?*

If a wife/woman was cooking and she happened to drop her dish rag/cloth on the floor, someone was coming that was hungry and needed food to eat. Then immediately she would start cooking more food to be prepared for whoever the hungry person was. Note: She didn't think that dropping her dish cloth might have been because she was a little bit clumsy.

If a woman washed dishes by hand and she wet the front of her clothes with the dish water, then she would marry a drunkard, or her next husband would be a drunk (Gosh, I must have drowned myself in dish water). And if a woman already had the information beforehand on how to pick the right man, why would she deliberately marry a drunkard? After all, she had the pre-knowledge of wetting the front of her clothes with dish water, didn't she? Ok, ok, I was tricked by this tall, dark, and handsome country boy. Serves me right. I should have been sniffing his breath instead of looking in his gorgeous eyes.

If the moon was growing toward a full moon, then the farmers could not kill the animals for food because the meat would swell while cooking and never get tender enough to eat. Even if the pigs were ready to be slaughtered, they would have to wait for the moon to be

shrinking toward the last quarter to kill the meat for food so that the meat would be tender and juicy. Umm, so is that why some of the meats we buy from the supermarkets are so doggone tuff? The producers don't know when it's the proper time to kill the animals!

If you have bad scary dreams at night, it was because you ate pork meat or pork cracklings before going to bed. Because you ate it, when you awoke from your dream, you will not remember what the bad dream was about. Note: Why did it have to be pork? Couldn't it have been that the bad dream could have been caused by the stresses of that day? Maybe the animal wasn't killed at the proper time and is now haunting you. Ummm, think about that for a while.

If the sun comes out while it is raining, then the devil is beating his wife, but if it is raining hard while the sun is shining, then that means the devil is getting a good beating from his wife (my sister-in-law Geraldine's input). Note: Where did this logic come from? If the devil and his wife can't get along with each other, then they should have gotten a divorce, or maybe they did. That's why he is down here messing around in our marriages and businesses.

He's unhappy and wants all of us to be unhappy also. Watch out for that devil!

If you look up at sky and see the moon during the daytime, then you were a lazy, *sorry* person. You were to keep your head down with your eyes on your work and not the sky. As a child, I was told to help my grandmother chop the grass out of the garden. This means we had to remove the grass from the vegetables to allow them to grow. When I became tired, I would stop chopping to look up into the sky. I loved looking at the sky because I loved guessing what the clouds resembled. I would say, "Look, Mama, I see the moon." She would never stop chopping but would tell me that I did not see the moon. Then she would say, "Gurl, stop lookin' in dat sky an git bac ta wok caws tain't no moon in dat sky in da middle of da day." Note: She just wanted me to keep working so we could finish our work sooner. It took me years to realize her logic because I knew I saw the moon in the daytime. I wasn't crazy, but I had better not tell her I saw it!

Now listen to this one. If you hear a bird tweeting in a tree early in the morning, you should understand what he was saying to you. He was singing, "laziness will kill you, laziness will, kill you, laziness will kill you," according to what my sister-in-law was told by her forefathers. Note: Now please tell me who in this world has heard a simple bird give that kind of message! Could it have been that the bird knew the secrets men tried to hide from their neighbors, or maybe the birds were warning the person that they knew what they had done that night before and was trying to tell someone else their secrets. You see, in my great and grandparents' day, the men were always sneaking in other men's back door. That is why everyone in the country are sisters, brothers, and cousins.

If the first of the month came in like a lamb (warm, calm, and gentle), then it would go out like a lion (cold, windy, and stormy), especially the month of March and vice versa. Note: I believed this because I told you my grandfather, Papa, was a predictor of the weather and time (farmer astrologist). I would look at him in amazement when he would look at the sun and tell us, accurately, what time of the day it was, when it was going to rain, or when a bad storm was coming our way. Therefore, I believed what he said.

If Christmas weather was warm, then there will be hot graveyards the next year (many people die), but if it is a cold Christmas, the graveyards will be cold (not many people dying). Note: This saying is puzzling because people are dying whether warm or cold. Those that are not dying naturally are being killed by the newly named viruses, law officers who have sworn to protect us, and from the teenagers who are killing each other over nonsense things, and, also, the effects of political wars in other nations. Killings of any of God's creations must grieve His heart because it sure grieves mine. In the years 2021-2022, everyday news reporters inform us of someone killing someone else, lawfully and unlawfully. The devil is happy because his kingdom is becoming enlarged every day. The scriptures give us the solution in 2 Chronicles 7:14 NIV, "If my people, who are called by my name, will humble themselves and pray and seek my face and turn from their wicked ways, then will I hear from heaven, and I will forgive their sin and **I will heal their land**." Everybody, this land needs a healing, from top leaders in government, to the peons, and to the least of these.

If it is a full moon, then you could expect all sorts of crazy things to happen, especially the people who have mental problems and the elderly in nursing homes. They would act unusual and erratic during this time and calm the rest of the days of the month. Note: This saying used to seem valid back then, but now, many people are acting and doing crazy things, not just the old and mentally challenged, and it has nothing to do with a full moon, either. Why can't we have peace, justice, joy, and love toward our sisters and brothers of every nation and ethnic background?

If you saw the birds flying north, then it would be warm weather in that region where the flight originated, then if you saw birds flying south, they are leaving cold weather to return to a warmer climate. Note: That makes sense because if some people could migrate like birds, they would pack up and go to wherever the weather is that pleased them. When I decided to leave Baltimore, the entire state was iced over and cold. I did like the birds, I moved South!

If it rains a lot during fall and winter months, the crops would be withered, poor, and wouldn't produce, but if it rained a little, the crops would be healthy and plentiful. Note: This is true because if it rains too much during the fall months, the fields were too wet to plant seedling in the spring, or the farmers could not get in the fields to plant on due time. If they were able to plant in wet soil and when the seedling would begin to grow, the baby plants would drown and wither and there would be no crops to harvest that year. I am a witness. We hardly had food to carry us through that year. God's mercy showed up and showed out. He kept making a way for us and we always had a home-cooked biscuit or cornbread to eat. Of course, I had to fight my five brothers to get one biscuit because they would grab five biscuits at one time to put on their plates. Then they guarded their plates by putting their arms around their plates, as if they were guarding Fort Knox to keep their biscuits safe from their siblings' tactics to get one of them.

If you plant your seedlings on a light night (moon shining bright) then the bugs and worms would come and eat the crops during the night, but if you plant on a dark night (moon not shing bright), the bugs would leave your seedlings alone to flourish. Note: My grandparents used to determine when the moon was brightly shinning on a clear night or was covered by clouds by studying the *Farmers' Almanac*. The *Farmers' Almanac* was the farmers' Bible.

If you walked under a ladder while it was leaning against a wall, it was bad luck. You had to walk backward under the ladder, then walk in front of it to go to your destination. Note: I cannot explain this one. Evidently, they only knew how to farm, but then, that doesn't make sense because they had to build their houses to live in them! Maybe it could have begun with a safety concern. Who knows?

If you drove past a graveyard and pointed your finger toward it, then your finger would rot off if you did not bite your finger first before you put in in the pocket of your pants (sister-in-law, Geraldine). You had to make sure your hand stayed in your lap or in your pockets while passing the graveyard. Note: This really scared me. Who wanted their fingers to rot off because you pointed your finger at a graveyard? Of course, I never saw proof that someone had ever lost a finger. I was always afraid to pass a graveyard because for entertainment, my grandfather would tell us a story of how he used to pass the graveyard with his horse and buggy. Just before he got to the graveyard, he would look back and see a ghost with no head sitting on the back of his wagon. When he got in front of the graveyard, the headless ghost would hop off the back of the wagon and go back in the grave. That story would have me so afraid until I could not go to my bedroom. When I got in bed, I could not sleep for seeing that headless ghost going into the graveyard. Even though we were crying and pleading, he would not allow my sister and I to go into their bedroom at night. I guess my grandfather thought the story was funny, but it was devastating to my sister and me. My grandma began keeping a low light on in our room at night. To this day, I cannot sleep in a dark room.

If you were eating, or if you sneezed while eating food, and the food fell from your mouth, then you would get the news of someone you knew had died, according to my first mother-in-law, Martha. Then to keep your acquaintances from dying, you had to make sure you chewed with your mouth closed. Note: Well, you should have been chewing with your mouth closed anyhow because no one wants to see chewed-up food hanging out of someone's mouth, ugh.

If a child got chicken pox, a sure way of curing it was to send the child into the hen house and let the chickens fly over the child's head. It would dry up the chicken pox immediately, according to my grandma, Sarah. Note: I don't know if this was true because my grandma made me go into the hen house when I had chicken pox and I still had to suffer through it. Today, very few people have chicken coops, but you can

Google it to see where you can take your children to have the chickens fly over their heads to cure them of chicken pox if they ever get it. You may save a doctor's bill!!!

If you were born with a gap between your two front teeth, then you were a born liar. Note: Society cannot spot a born liar today because dental specialists have invented the means of closing gaps between teeth, such as braces and liners. Today, no one can spot a liar, according to our forefathers. Of course, I was born with a large gap that would have caused me to seek psychological help, if we could have afforded it back then. My brothers tortured me constantly about the gap between my teeth. I could have been scarred for life had I not been so defiant. Therefore, I prayed to

God to help me to always tell the truth, but I forgot to ask Him to help me not to steal.

Wait, wait, wait. Let me tell you what I stole. During the late summer and early fall, my mom would can bushels of peaches in quart mason jars. I loved peaches, but she would always say we could not eat them until late winter. I said, "Yes ma'am." Those peaches looked so good in those jars, and they just kept calling my name. I convinced my sister that if we stole a jar and she ate half the quart and I ate the other half, then Mama would never know. She agreed and we ate peaches every day for a week. The last day of the week, my sister decided she was tired of peaches and would not help me eat the other half of the jar of peaches I had opened. What was I to do with the other half because I was too full to eat the rest of the jar of peaches?

I decided I would hide them behind all the full jars of peaches in the pantry. You can guess what happened next. After a few days, I had forgotten I had hidden the half jar of peaches. Mama decided to do an inventory of her stock, and what did she find? Yes, the half jar of peaches. She began to do her detective work, CIA, and asked, "Who did it?" I had always been afraid of a beating. I did not get the punishment because she concluded that maybe she just did not have enough peaches on that day to fill the jar and left it half full. I was so relieved that she blamed herself until it cured my desire and taste for peaches. They still looked pretty in those jars, but I did not touch those things again. No, sir; never again, the risk was too great!

If a young girl developed breasts before she became a teenager, she was considered too fast around boys, promiscuous. Then the parents had to make sure they kept an eye on her, watched her every move around boys. Of course, who began to develop early? You guessed it, ME. I did my best not to let the front of my blouses give my secret away, but they did anyhow. Note: Oh boy, my grandparents would turn over in their graves if they had to watch the young girls of today! They would spend all their time spying to make sure the bosomed girl was not talking to the boys in the neighborhood. If I had let all the negative things that were predicted over my life as a child affect my adult life, I would be lying on a psychiatrist's couch as we speak. Glory to God, He has kept my mind.

Listen to this: A carry-on from the previous saying, if a young woman wore her dress or skirt too tight and short and her blouse so low that the top of her breasts showed, her father would tell her to go back and get dressed and say to her, "You got to have some shameness 'bout yourself," according to my sister-in-law Dena's father. Note: What has happened to the "shameness" that today's young ladies are supposed to have? The shorter the dress, the lower the blouse, and the tighter the jeans, the better they like it. There is nothing left for the young men's imagination because they see all that is supposed to be the private parts of the young girls and some older women, too. God, help all our women who think that this is the proper way to dress.

If you had a dream the night before, and it was a good dream, then you could not tell anyone about the dream before nightfall on that same day because if you did, then the dream would not come true. Note: Oh shucks! None of mine come true anyway, whether I tell someone before nightfall or any other time of day. There are some I know I would not want to tell nor come to pass, especially the one where I wouldn't dare to tell anyone and have to ask God to forgive me for the sinful illusions. I realized what my parents meant when they used to say, "sweet dreams."

If you were born with black or dark gums, and out of anger, you bite someone, then the person you bit would surely die because your gums were poisonous. That's why they are black. Note: Whether that statement is true or not, I do not know. My mom kept all eleven of us at home, in the country, until we finished high school. Since she did not allow us to fight each other, I did not have a candidate to try out my poisonous gum bites on to see if what my grandparents had said was true. If it was true, then there are a lot of people I would like to bite, for real!

The police caught this man stealing. This older man looked at the man to observe his actions. Then he said, "Oh, he's guilty alright. He is jest as nervous as a long-tail cat sitting under Grandma's rocking chair and she's a rocking in it," from my sister-in-law Dena's father." Note: What kind of expression was this crook displaying? Are cats really that dumb just to sit and wait for Grandma to rock on their tails? I don't have a cat because cats are sneaky and can't be trained like someone can train a puppy. I hear they are finicky, whatever that means. I think this is a dumb thief to steal something then wait to be caught. The modern-day thief would be long gone before the policemen got on the scene and when caught, would deny stealing anything even with the evidence still in his pockets.

If anyone combed their hair on the outside of their house—porch in the old days (it was too hot inside the house)—and a bird just happened to grab a piece of their hair and used it to make a nest, then that person, who the hair belonged to, would begin to have terrible migraine headaches and eventually go completely crazy or insane. Note: I do not believe this saying but, is that why beauticians make sure everyone's hair is put in trash bags and secured tightly? The actions of some people cause me to think that birds have found a lot of people's hair in these trash bags and made bird nests. If you do not believe me, just look around at what's going on in the world. Almost everybody has gone off their rockers and want to bring other innocent people along with them. God, have mercy on your people!

Speaking about hair, if a person wanted to hurt you without you knowing who that person was, that person could get a piece of your hair, then they could work roots on you using your hair to make you go crazy and confused. Then they could do whatever they wanted to do to you without you knowing what happened to you, according to my ex-mother-in-law, Martha Lawrence. Note: If someone combs or cuts your hair, make sure you collect every strand of hair, take it home with you, and burn it to make sure no strands of your hair fall into the wrong hands. Note: Everybody goes to hair salons these days. Do you think that's why people are so crazy? Are they crazy because someone took their hair and used magic potions on it to cause people to be so selfish, destructive, mean, and evil?

Next time you go to your hair salon, be sure to gather all your hair and take it home with you. I would not want it to get in the wrong hands.

If you hear a dog howling at the moon during the daytime hours, then surely before nightfall you will hear of someone's death who was close to you, or a neighbor. Note: I live in the city where people keep their dogs in their homes; therefore, I do not hear dogs howling, but I have heard of plenty of deaths of the people who were close to me. Conclusion: The howling does not matter whether I hear it or not, people are dying every day. Maybe because dogs are kept inside, they howl just to get outside, and it has nothing to do with whether someone dies or not. It's all about the dog's agenda and how he wants to conduct himself for that particular day and hour. Give the dog a break and let God's will be done.

Since I am talking about animals, let me inform you that if a rooster crows before you get out of bed in the morning, then you are a lazy, sorry person, and your life will only come to ruins because you will fail in every effort to be successful. Note: What the heck does getting up before the rooster crows have to do with your success in life? I think that was the ploy of those huge plantation owners to make sure that farm workers started their day before dawn only to end after sunset. Times have surely changed. My parents used to tell us if we had a job that required us to be at work by 9 a.m., then those were bankers' hours, and they did not trust bankers. They put their money under a mattress and the women put their money in their bosoms to keep it safe. That was the safest place in the world because if anyone tried to put their hands down their bosoms, they were in for a knockdown, drag-out fight. That statement meant that whoever tried would leave laying down on the back end of a mule and wagon just barely breathing.

You dishonor Jesus if you washed your sheets between December 24th and January 6th, New Christmas and Old Christmas, because Jesus was wrapped in swaddling clothes (sheets) and He is worthy to be worshipped and honored, per my grandmother, Sarah Daniels. Therefore, if a child peed on his/her sheets during this time and season, too bad. They had to wait until after January 6th to get clean sheets. Oh boy, did we have to keep our noses pinched a lot of times during that week!

If someone swept your feet with a broom, then you would never get married, but you could stop that curse by spitting on the broom. If you did not get married, then you would go to jail, whichever was the worst curse. During that time, if you happened to sweep someone's feet, they would chase you down until you could not run any longer, just to spit on the broom. Nobody wanted to marry, and nobody surely wanted to go to jail, per my sister-in-law, Geraldine Bell, told by her father.

If you married a city slicker, someone reared in the city, your marriage would be miserable and unhappy, then you would have to find a country farm boy who would make you happy and father lots of children. Quick story. A gentleman stopped by my mother-in-law's house to inquire about her oldest son and asked her directions to his house. Warning, during this time, asking directions to find someone in the country was like pulling teeth. My mother-in-law tried her best to tell the gentleman how to find her son's house. Finally, she said, "When you see a house with a lot of chillen running round barefoot, dats the house." She gave him the right information about the yard full of children, but I don't know if he found where her son lived or not. I do know the man did not come back for further directions.

I know why the men did not want the women to hear their conversation, because they used to brag, "If you keep a woman bigged, with a bun in her oven (pregnant), and barefooted, then you won't have to worry about her leaving you. She will be satisfied staying at home barefooted." I have always said that God was biased in our punishment because of what Adan and Eve did in the Garden of Eden by eating the forbidden fruit. When He punished Eve by her bearing children, I think He should have made it equal. He should have had it so that every other year, it would be the man's turn to have babies. If He had done that, I would have made sure that when it came time for my husband to bear fruit, I would have given him the whole tree full. I bet you if that were the case, the world would not be overpopulated now. Men cannot bear to have a lot of pain without complaining.

If you let your cow eat wild onions, then the milk they gave would taste like onions. Cows eat all kinds of stuff, why did it not taste like grass or the feed they ate? I can imagine if marijuana was popular back then, they would let the cows eat it. The cows would be staggering all over the place and all the babies would be drug addicts from drinking the milk the cows produced. At least they would not have to worry about babies crying from colic. The babies would be too high to feel the discomfort.

That joker so sorry, he won't work in a pie stoe tastin' pies. I suppose my forefathers thought that tasting pies in a store was a prestigious occupation and it was easy to perform. In their day, if a person did not work, he was the lowest of the lowest in social status of the neighborhood. In fact, the Bible teaches us in the King James Bible found in 2 Thessalonians 3:10: "For even when we were with you, we commanded you this: if anyone will not work, neither shall he eat." I understand this scripture in this way, "If a man doesn't work, he surely won't eat the food I bought for my consumption, if he is able to work but refuses to work." It was true then and it is true now. If he is too sorry to work at some kind of job, let him starve!

If you don't stand up for something, then you will fall for anything, especially if there is a matter of deciding what is right and what is wrong. Being an upright person means that one must decide the validity on righteous matters and be willing to stand or support the decision you made. My grandparents used to say you were being wishy-washy when you can't make up your mind on anything. Revelations 3:15-16 of the Bible talks about what happens when you are lukewarm, neither hot nor cold. It says that God will spur you out of His mouth and so should your associates.

If you have shifty eyes, then you are up to no good. Having shifty eyes, not looking someone in their eyes when talking to someone, is a learned condition taught during slavery of Black people. Teaching the slaves not to look in the slave owners' eyes was part of the oppression and control over them. As slaves were freed from slavery, the control was broken, and they began to look people in their eyes while talking to someone. Nowadays, people believe it is ill-mannered to talk to someone without looking them in their eyes and shows you have something to hide. You can tell a lot about someone by looking in their eyes because discernment kicks in to determine your sincerity and truthfulness in what you say.

As children playing, someone would tell us if we stepped on a crack on the ground, we would break our daddy's back and if we stepped on a line, then our mamas drank wine, per my sister-in-law, Geraldine. That was so scary to us because none of us wanted to hurt our daddies and it was a disgrace if our mamas drank wine during our childhood. I don't know where the saying originated, but it was psychologically distressing to us as children. We were devastated if we happened to step on a crack or line because the other children would start to chant, "Ohhh, your mama drink wine," which caused us to fight like the lives of our mamas depended on us winning the fight.

If you saw big black or brown caterpillars crawling on the ground, then it was going to be bad weather. I don't know about bad weather, but it was bad for me. They sent me screaming, from the top of my lungs, for someone to come and rescue me from those creatures. Thinking about those large hairy looking creatures gives me chills, even at my age.

If a man's wife was not doing her wifely duties as she was supposed to do, his father would give his son this advice, "Son, I wouldn't stay with that woman as long as spit would stay on a red-hot stove," as Dena's father would tell his sons. In modern days, it would be the women following that advice because we also bring home the bacon. I don't think there are too many women who serve it up in a pan. This marriage thing is a two-way street. You do, I do, we all do together. We should have never been introduced to women's liberation and rights a while ago. We have been liberated and we won't turn back to the old way of doing things. Equal rights for equal benefits in the workplace and in the home.

In my grandparents' day, everything was useful. If anyone was seen with dry skin, they would say that that person needed to put some fried meat grease (bacon grease) on their skin because their skin looked a rough as a corn cob. I went to school many days smelling and looking like I had fallen into a lard can. It wasn't too embarrassing because the other children looked and smelled the same as I did.

If they saw a pregnant woman, they would say, "Uhm, some man done knocked her up or she done gone and put a roll in that oben (oven)." How degrading! I suppose the woman got pregnant all by herself. It's likened to the woman in the Bible who was caught in the very act of adultery who was taken to Jesus (John 8:3-11). The men asked Jesus what should be done to her because the law said she was to be stoned to death. They took the woman, but where was the man she was adulterating with? He should have been stoned also. She could not commit adultery alone. Jesus fixed them all. He said, "He without sin, cast the first stone." All the men left with their tails between their legs. When Jesus stood up from writing on the ground, only He and the woman were standing there.

If a person was doing things that society did not think they should be behaving, saying, or doing, they would say,

"That person sho need ta git sum ligon (religion) or they wouldn't be doing that there thang."

This saying is good advice, "Huny, use need ta keep yore friends clos ta you but keep yore enemy closer." This advice meant that you should keep both groups of people near you in order to watch their activities. In watching their activities, they cannot do you harm without you being aware of what they were doing. In other words, you would not be caught by surprise when they try to do something to hurt you. My ex-mother-in-law, Martha, used to say, "You will neber kill me and I be lookin' rat at chu."

If someone were to give you something you needed and it wasn't quite what you expected, you were not to reject the offer because they would quickly tell you, "A begger can't be choosey and you had better be grateful for what they gave you in da furst place." In fact, my mom used to tell us, "If you don't want that, give it back and I will give you something better." We, as children, would give back what she originally had given us. She would take it back and not give us anything in return. Our feelings would be so hurt, but she would not give it back even when tears were rolling down our cheeks. We learned how to accept whatever she offered to us.

We grew all the vegetables and fruits and raised almost everything we ate, including meats. Our parents did not let the grapes grow on single poles but allowed them grow on overhead beds. They would tell the young girls not to go under the grapevines  because it would make us "lose all our hair." No girl wanted to be baldheaded. I believe they told us that because they did not want us under the grapevine while the boys were under there. Parents were protective of their girls and prevented them from having contact with boys until they thought it was proper for girls to start dating. Not only that, but I also have alopecia, hair loss. Evidently, I must have been hardheaded and went under the grapevine anyway.

On New Year's Day, it was bad luck if a man did not enter anyone's house before a woman entered. Then to have good luck, a man would enter through the front door and leave through the back door. After that, all other people were welcomed to visit, including the first man that entered the door. Now that I look back on those days, I believe my grandpa kept a stash of liquor around the barn because he would not allow my sister, Vera, and I to go there. All the men would come back to the house with smaller than usual eyes, laughing, talking, and telling scary stories. We knew something had happened while they visited the barn, but we didn't know what had happened. Children were not allowed to be in "grown folks' business" back then.

Our forefathers made sure everyone had a coin, some money, in our pockets on

New Year's Day, because if we did not have money on New Year's, then we would be poor the rest of the year. Evidently, we never had money in our pockets on New Year's Day or the old saying did not work, because we were always in need of money every day of the year. We survived by the grace of God.

Our parents always made us wear a coat or a sweater in the winter because they told us if we did not wear one, we would catch cold in our "hindparts" or "hinyhole." If we happened to have a sniffle, they would say, "I told you to keep that coat on. Now you got a cold in your hindparts. Now, com en tak dis castor oil." Oh! How I hated that nasty stuff. I had no choice but to swallow it because my grandma would stand over us

66

with a switch in her hand, daring us to spit it out of our mouths. She could not afford to buy more of it. I would rather swallow that killer oil than to get my legs switched.

It did not matter how hard we worked on the farm, we could not complain of back pain because they would say, "You ain't got no back, yungun. You only gotta grizcle, the cartilage between the bones that were not bones yet." I thought to myself, because I dared not say it out loud, *I don't care what it is called but my back hurts*. We were not allowed to complain about any sicknesses, not even a headache. Sometimes what they told us sounded harsh, but I suppose it was to make us stronger to bear life's struggles as adults, and it has.

On the first snowfall of the winter each year, we were told to go outside barefoot and walk around for a while, then go back inside. That act would shield us from catching a cold the rest of the winter. I suppose it worked because to this day, I do not have colds, never had the flu or pneumonia. Thank you, Mama, for all your home remedy cures.

For years, I felt guilty about sleeping in bed past 5:30 a.m. When I got married, I thought it would be different living with my in-laws. No, there was no difference. My mother-in-law, Martha Lawrence, would start yelling about the same time in the morning as my mama did. Just before the rooster crowed, she would start yelling, "Y'all git out dat der beed wit' yore lazy, sorry self, lettin' da sun bake biskits in yore hindparts, and com ta eat this hear teat foe its git cold." Maybe some of you can decipher what she meant by saying that. I still don't get the meaning. We knew she meant for us to get out of bed immediately, and we did. Who wanted to eat that early in the morning, anyhow? My brother-in-law would be sitting at the table nodding. Sometimes, his head would almost fall in his plate, and my mother-in-law would slap him on the back of his head to wake him up. She would tell him that he should have gone to bed earlier. How much earlier could we have gone to bed? Because we were in bed by the time the sun set in the west.

Speaking of my mother-in-law, she would never complain of pain, but she would always say "I have a misery" in whatever body part was bothering her at a particular time. I decided to research "misery," and it means a source of great discomfort of mind and body. She described her pain, exactly, because she had many life struggles that were very painful and distressing. I met her in her old age, but she was still a strong woman who worked in the fields, went home to cook three meals a day, washed clothes by hand, scrubbed her floors on her knees, ironed all wearable clothes including her husband's underwear, and expected me to do the same. NOT IN THIS LIFETIME! She was not educated but she was wise in the many things in life that tried to knock us down. God gives wisdom to all who want to be successful in whatever area of life, with or without formal education. She just "knew things."

Her husband and sons were above average hunters and fishermen. They would come home after a day of hunting, tired and ready to eat. No man was allowed to wear a hat or cap inside the house. Wearing a hat inside was considered being disrespectful and it would bring bad luck to the inhabitants of that house. It was damnation to that man who happened to forget and lay his hat on the kitchen table! My mother-in-law slapped the back of her son's head many times for doing just that thing. He would continue to eat as if she had not slapped him at all. Evidently, he was a slow learner or did not care about that superstition, but that scene entertained me many times; it was hilarious.

No adult I knew cursed or called God's name in vain, whether angry or not. The most curse words they would say when they made an error was, "dab blame it," or, "gots ta be moe karful (I got to be more careful.)." I made the mistake of saying "dog gone it." My mom was very upset and told me that I "might as well cuss." I remember one day my brother, Leroy, came home from school excited because he had learned a new word that he had heard his teacher say. He decided to use the word and therefore, proceeded to call my brother, Howard, a heifer. A heifer is a baby calf, but he did not know that and neither did Howard. Howard went running to Mama to tell her that Leroy had called him a bad name. The CIA proceeded to investigate what possessed Leroy to even think of a bad word. Mama asked Howard what was the bad word that he had been called, and he answered, "Heifer." Oh! My goodness! I thought my mom was going to faint. She asked Leroy what a heifer was and, of course, he had no idea what a heifer was. She told him if he did not tell her what it was she was going to beat his lips until he told her. The scary thing about that was, she meant to do just that. He could not tell her what a heifer was because, after all, he had only heard it from his teacher, and he dared not ask him what it was either. He just knew that the word sounded like something he could repeat. Needless to say, Leroy went to school the next day with swollen lips. Note: All of us learned that repeating what someone has said can get you in deep trouble. We were not dumb. If one sibling got in trouble for doing something, we knew not to repeat what they had done, or if we did, we knew we would receive the same punishment. Mama did not play!

My coworker in Jesus, Mother Elizabeth Berry, and I were conversating after church when we began talking about our children's pet dogs. She told me of how one of the new pets would cry and yelp all night until she gave him peanut butter. I was puzzled and asked why she gave the dog peanut butter. She explained that giving the dog peanut butter would stop his crying because the peanut butter would stick to his mouth and teeth. The dog would have to stop wailing to work at getting rid of the peanut butter from his mouth. Note: I thought that was so cruel, but if peanut butter is that "dangerous" to dogs, should people eat it? Another thought, maybe we should give more to humans because some humans don't know when to stop yelping their mouths either, especially church folk! Oops, did I say that?

"Notes"

Since I have started meddling in other people's business, it's time for me to close this session. More of traveling down memory lane with my forefathers and mothers will be revealed at a later time. Maybe I will throw in some old medical remedies from Dr. Grandpa in my next edition. Blessings, keep smiling, and remember the Proverbs of our past.

The End

www.ingramcontent.com/pod-product-compliance
Lightning Source LLC
Chambersburg PA
CBHW072209090426
42740CB00012B/2445